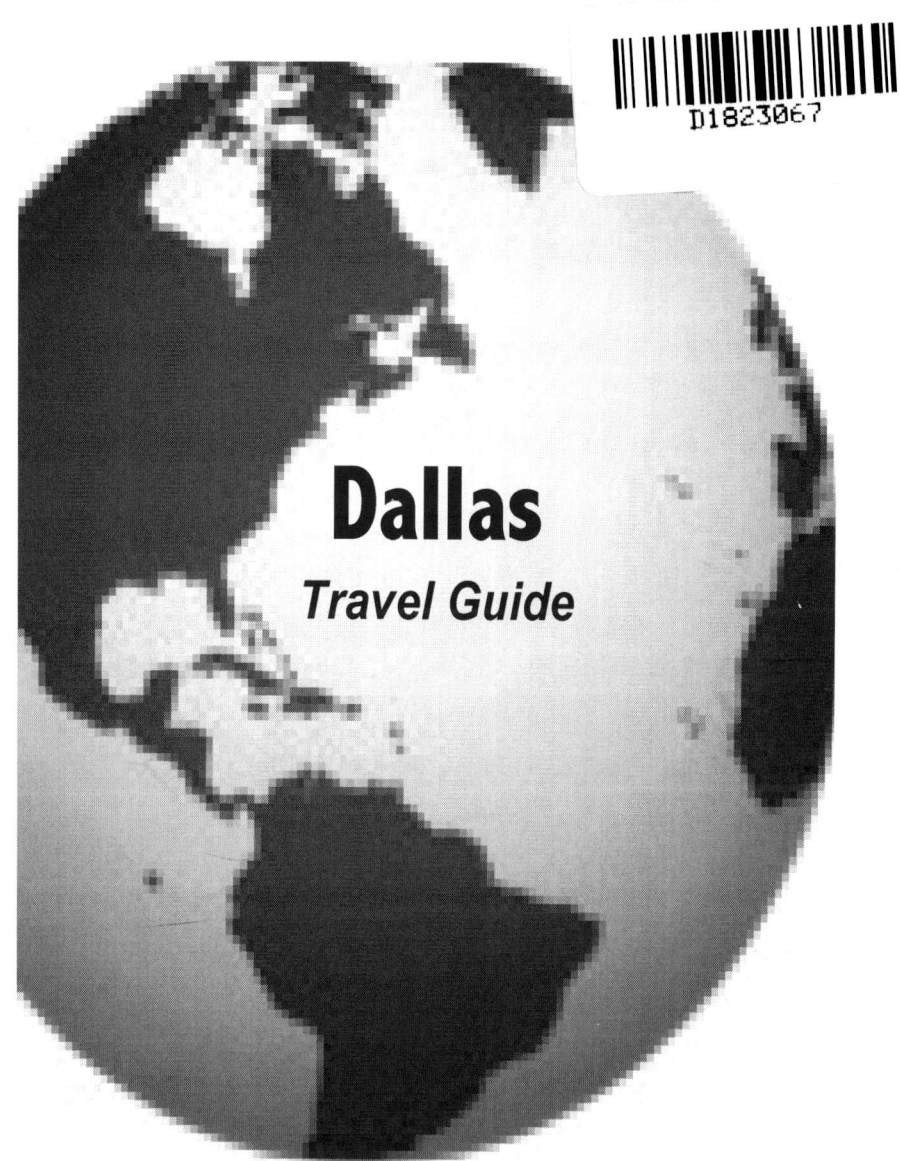

Dallas
Travel Guide

Quick Trips Series

Table of Contents

BUDGET TIPS   39

KNOW BEFORE YOU GO   53

Dallas

Dallas is the ninth-largest city in the United States and is the third-largest city in the state of Texas (after Houston and San Antonio). Moderate weather, southern hospitality, world-class restaurants, and leading sporting events are just a few of Dallas' tourist attractions. The city has the largest urban art district in the country and is a melting pot of diversity with many lifestyles, cultures, and religions living peacefully in this Texan powerhouse.

Dallas covers 343 square miles (888 square km) and has a population of 1.2 million people. It is one of the most popular convention cities in the country given its ability to entertain and accommodate visitors at reasonable prices. This modern and sophisticated city attracts visitors from around the world.

🌐 Customs & Culture

To understand Dallas, you should first explore the history of the state of Texas. Before the Spanish explorers declared Texas as a Spanish territory, the area that is now Dallas was occupied by the Native American Caddo people. Until 1821, when Mexico won its independence from Spain, it remained under Spanish rule. Then in 1836,

DALLAS TRAVEL GUIDE

Texas broke off from Mexico to become its own independent nation, the Republic of Texas. For nine years, until 1845 when it became an official state, Texas was independent. This sense of pride and originality is still proudly displayed to this very day.

In 1856, Dallas was incorporated as an official city. Politically, it is very conservative with Protestant Christianity as its most popular religion. Although the city has long been associated with oil, the resource is not actually found within the city. But Dallas has a very strong economic influence not only on its state of Texas, but on the United States as well. It is seen as a city of opportunity and has many Fortune 500 companies.

Although Dallas has been mostly a Caucasian city since its birth, cultural diversity has increased over the 20th

DALLAS TRAVEL GUIDE

Century. Like much of Texas, Dallas' largest minority group is Hispanic, due to its proximity to Mexico. There is a strong African-American presence in the south of Dallas and in the northwest. Throughout the city, however, there are localized groups of Korean, Chinese, German, Indian, Taiwanese, Polish, Russian, and Middle Eastern groups.

The culture of the city is portrayed by its many festivals and events. Its annual Cinco de Mayo festivities are represented by the strong Mexican population. St. Patrick's Day is celebrated by both the city's Irish and those who are only Irish for a day. Other festivals include the Greek Food Festival of Dallas and the State Fair of Texas - the second of which is the state's largest event, bringing in over $350 million to the economy of Texas.

🌎 Geography

Dallas is one of the most accessible cities in America due to its central location. DFW International Airport, is the fourth busiest in the world. As such a large city, it is easier to break it up into sections in order to get your bearings. Downtown Dallas is located in "Central Dallas" and has a number of districts itself; including, the West End Historic District, the Main Street District, the Arts District, the Convention Center District, and more.

"East Dallas" is where Deep Ellum is located, a very trendy and artsy area near downtown. The Munger Place Historic District is located here as well, a district that has a significant number of Frank Lloyd Wright-style homes. Preston Hollow is also in East Dallas and is known for its extravagant homes and high end shopping centers that include NorthPark Center, Galleria Dallas, and Highland Park Village.

"South Dallas" has seen high rates of poverty and crime. There is undeveloped land aplenty, compared to other areas of Dallas, as a result of years of slow growth in the area. Just southwest of Downtown sits Oak Cliff, which is mostly Hispanic but also African American and Native American. There are a few hotspots in "South Dallas" that include a neighborhood called, The Cedars: an area much loved by eclectic artists. Fair Park is also in South Dallas and is where the Texas State Fair calls home.

A newer area of Dallas that is currently seeing new development is "Midtown Dallas." This is a modern area located between University Park, Preston Hollow,

Lakewood, and Uptown. It is here where you will find

newer high-rise apartments and shopping centers.

🌐 Weather & Best Time to Visit

Dallas has a climate that is "humid subtropical." This

means hot and humid summers with mild and cool

winters. Although summer brings humidity, dry winds from

the west and the north can shoot temperatures well past

100 °F (38 °C). When it is humid, the heat-humidity

indexes can reach 117 °F (47 °C). These high

temperatures make Dallas one of the hottest cities in the

United States during the summer.

A typical winter day in Dallas is sunny with a high of 63 °F

(17 °C) and a low of 36 °F (2 °C). But when "Blue

Northers" (strong cold fronts) pass through the area,

nightly lows can plummet past 25 °F (−4 °C) for a few

days with daytime highs struggling to pass 40 °F (4 °C).

Dallas doesn't see much snowfall but usually sees a

couple days of it per year, averaging 1.8 inches (4.6 cm).

Pleasant times to visit Dallas are spring and autumn. The

weather is more volatile during these seasons, however,

with severe storms and tornado threats on occasion.

Dallas' primary weather threat is tornadoes, as the city

sits in the heart of "Tornado Alley."

Sights & Activities: What to See & Do

🌐 Dallas Arboretum & Botanical Gardens

8525 Garland Road, Dallas, TX 75218 (East Dallas)

(214) 515-6500

http://www.dallasarboretum.org/

Sixty-six acres of beautiful outdoor gardens create the

DALLAS TRAVEL GUIDE

Dallas Arboretum and Botanical Gardens in its pristine setting on White Rock Lake.

Visitors to the Arboretum are able to enjoy concerts, art shows, educational opportunities, and seasonal outdoor festivals. The Arboretum has been named one of the best places in the world for viewing spring flowers. It is a relaxing oasis in a large metropolis of skyscrapers and general city life.

The history of the Arboretum began in the early 1930s with a vision from Everette DeGolyer. However, it wasn't until 1984 that the Arboretum opened to the public. Visitors can tour the DeGolyer Home, a Latin Colonial Revival style home built for him and his wife in 1939. The house is massive, covering 21,000 square feet (1950 square meters).

Two restaurants sit on the property: the Lulu Mae Slaughter Dining Terrace and the DeGolyer House.

The Arboretum is open daily from 9 a.m. until 5 p.m. Costs for admission are as follows:

Adults (13-64) $15

Seniors (65+) $12

Children (3-12) $10

Onsite Parking $10

🌐 Zero Gravity Thrill Amusement Park

11131 Malibu Dr., Dallas, TX 75229

(972) 484-8359

http://www.gojump.com/

DALLAS TRAVEL GUIDE

One of the top attractions for thrill seekers is Zero Gravity Thrill Amusement Park. They feature extreme rides that include bungee jumping from seven stories, a skycoaster more than 100 feet off the ground, the "Texas Blastoff" that propels riders straight in the air at 70 mph, and "Nothing But Net" which is a 16 story free fall.

Zero Gravity may be an extreme park for thrill seekers but it is also proud of its perfect safety record, making visitors feel as safe as possible, even when plunging through the air several stories above the ground.

All of the rides at Zero Gravity Dallas are priced per rider. Each first ride is $32.99 plus tax. Each consecutive ride is $14.99 more.

Park hours vary, depending on the time of year and day of the week. Typically, the park is open from 4 – 10 p.m. on weeknights, noon until midnight on weekends, and noon until 10 p.m. on Sundays.

Dallas World Aquarium

1801 North Griffin Street, Dallas, TX 75202

(214) 720-2224

http://www.dwazoo.com/

The Dallas World Aquarium is a must-see attraction when visiting the city. Be warned that most visitors and residence would agree, making it a bit crowded at times. Visiting as early in the day as possible will ensure you shorter waits in line, if any, and easier access to the exhibits.

DALLAS TRAVEL GUIDE

Visitors to the Dallas World Aquarium get the chance to not only walk through the Aquarium itself, with hundreds of Indo-Pacific fishes; but also to walk through four more ecosystems: Mundo Maya, South Africa, Orinoco, and Borneo. This makes it less of an aquarium and more of a tropical zoo with its exotic birds, sloths, crocodiles, monkeys, penguins, and more.

The Dallas World Aquarium is well kept and has a helpful and knowledgeable staff. When visiting, be sure to attend one of the feedings or educational talks. Every Saturday and Sunday in the Mundo Maya exhibit, the Grupo Pakal's festive dance performances are featured with native music at 11:15 a.m., 12:00 p.m., 12:45 p.m., 1:30 p.m., 2:15 p.m., 3:00 p.m., and 3:45 p.m.

There are two different cafes on site and a nice restaurant, Eighteen-O-One.

The Dallas World Aquarium is open daily from 9 a.m. until 5 p.m. Admission is $20.95 + tax for adults, $12.95 + tax for children ages 3 – 12, and $16.95 + tax for seniors ages 60 and older.

🌐 Nasher Sculpture Center

2001 Flora St., Dallas, TX 75201 (Downtown Dallas)

(214) 242-5100

http://www.nashersculpturecenter.org/

The Nasher Sculpture Center represents Raymond D. Nasher's vision of a roofless outdoor museum for sculptures from the 20th Century. It is located downtown, also serving as a peaceful retreat for the public. There is now an indoor gallery as well as the outdoor sculpture garden.

The building literally looks like a museum without a roof, although there is a roof made of glass panes supported by thin rods. Natural light from outdoors illuminates the art space, while the lower level has another gallery for those sculptures that are sensitive to light. There is also an indoor atrium on this level which opens to a terraced garden outside.

The Nasher Sculpture Center is open daily from 11 a.m. until 5 p.m. except for Mondays. The admission for adults is $10. Seniors age 65 and older pay $7. Children ages 12 and under are free. The first Saturday of each month is free to all visitors. Admission prices include the free audio tour as well as admission to any special exhibits.

🌐 Dallas Museum of Art

1717 North Harwood, (Downtown) Dallas, TX 75201

(214) 922-1200

http://www.dm-art.org/

Since 1984, the Dallas Museum of Art (DMA) has been enjoying its "newer" location in the Downtown Dallas Arts District. The DMA is a major art museum with over 24,000 works of art dating back to 300 BC. The museum has a lot going on with a variety of programs and hands-on workshops for kids as well.

The DMA café is open from 11 a.m. until 4 p.m. on Tuesdays through Sundays, but many visitors simply pack a small picnic and enjoy lunch in the museum's sculpture garden. There are plenty of shaded tables and chairs available with waterfalls, making it a quiet oasis in the heart of Downtown Dallas.

On Thursday nights the Museum is the place to be. Drinks and live music are served in the atrium from 6 p.m. until 8 p.m.

The Dallas Museum of Art is open daily (except for Mondays) from 11 a.m. until 5 p.m. On Thursdays, they are open until 9 p.m. On the third Friday of every month (except for December), the museum offers Late Night Fridays when it stays open until midnight.

General admission is free and includes the collection galleries as well as most of the exhibitions. Special exhibitions cost $16 for adults and $14 for seniors ages 65 and older. Children ages 11 and under are free.

◍ White Rock Lake Park

8300 East Lawther Drive Dallas, TX 75218 (East Dallas)

(972) 622-7283

http://www.dallasparks.org/parks/whiterock.aspx

Centrally located in East Dallas is White Lake Park, a unique 1,015 acre city lake that offers a variety of activities to its visitors. Before being used as a public park, it was farmland owned by the Cox and Daniel families. The city of Dallas had their eyes on the land as a long term plan for water preservation. According to legend, the Daniel family owned the land where the lake is located and protested for two nights before allowing water to be released to the land, creating the lake. It served its purpose once established as a water source but also became a favorite recreational spot for the city.

Surrounding the lake is a park with a 9.3 mile trail (5.1 km²) for hiking or biking. Pack a picnic to enjoy in one of its numerous picnic spots. Try your hand at fishing on one of the lake's piers for bass, catfish, or sunfish. Or check out one of the events at the White Rock Bath House Cultural Center,

http://www.dallasculture.org/bathHouseCultureCenter

Although sailing is permitted on the lake, swimming and use of motorized boats was banned in the 1950s.

🌐 Dealey Plaza & Sixth Floor Museum (JFK Assassination Site)

500 Main Street, Dallas, TX 75202 (Downtown Dallas)

(214) 571-1000

http://www.jfk.org/

DALLAS TRAVEL GUIDE

On November 22, 1963, President John F. Kennedy was riding in a motorcade through the historic West End District past a small city park known as Dealey Plaza. It is here that the fatal shots which killed the President were fired by Lee Harvey Oswald. The site includes the former Texas School Book Depository which is located overlooking and in Dealey Plaza. These sites (along with the famous "grassy knoll") will always be associated with the assassination of JFK.

Located at the convergence of Elm Street, Commerce Street, and Main Street; Dealey Plaza was named after George Bannerman Dealey. Dealey (1859-1946), was a civic leader, as well as an early publisher of The Dallas Morning News. He was a campaigner for the revitalization of the area, and monuments dedicated to him still stand to this day, contrary to many tourists assumptions that the monuments are dedicated to the late President.

One of the buildings that borders Dealey Plaza is the Texas School Book Depository building. It was from this building that Oswald fired his fatal shots. There is also an area in the Plaza known as "the grassy knoll" where many believe that other shots were fired at the President.

Today, tourists visit the plaza in large numbers, which has the same street signs and lights that were used in 1963. There is a small plaque commemorating the assassination in the plaza, which was declared a National Historic Landmark District by the National Park Service in 1993.

DALLAS TRAVEL GUIDE

Besides the Plaza, tourists can also visit the Sixth Floor Museum which occupies the two top floors of the old Book Depository. It is from here that visitors can get the same view as Oswald when he fired his shots. The museum details the life and legacy of President Kennedy by using historic films, interpretive displays, and other artifacts.

The Sixth Floor Museum is open daily except for Thanksgiving and Christmas. Hours are 10 a.m. until 6 p.m. Tuesdays through Sundays and from noon until 6 p.m. on Mondays. It takes approximately 90 minutes to tour the museum in entirety.

The ticket price includes an audio guide and is $16 for adults, $14 for seniors (ages 65+), and $13 for children (ages 6-18).

🌐 Bishop Arts District

Intersection of Bishop Street and Davis Street in North Oak Cliff, Dallas

http://bishopartsdistrict.weebly.com/index.html

The Bishop Arts District is a small (by Texas standards) shopping district in the North Oak Cliff area of Dallas, home to more than 60 independent stores, bars, restaurants, coffee shops, art galleries, and theaters. The area itself is one of the most unique neighborhoods in Dallas. Besides its shopping and social scene, the district also hosts several events such as wine walks and other small festivals.

The restaurants are an eclectic mix of American, Brazilian, Greek, Hawaiian, Meso-American, Italian, and Japanese (sushi). Its stores and boutiques include a pet store, clothing stores, soap stores, home décor, and plenty of unique items you cannot find in large shopping malls. This is a growing area with a new apartment complex that just sprouted up in 2011 called Zang Triangle Luxury Apartments. The area also hosts the Oak Cliff Film Festival which continues to add to the culture of the district on an annual basis.

🌐 Texas Theater

231 West Jefferson Boulevard, Dallas, TX (214) 948-1546

http://thetexastheatre.com/

Also located in the Bishop Arts District is the Texas Theater, this is a historic landmark and was the movie theater that gained its fame from Lee Harvey Oswald, who was arrested in the theater after being suspected of killing President Kennedy and police officer J.D. Tippit in

1963. The theater hosts a variety of events as well as showing mainstream movies.

At its inception in 1931, the theater was considered to be the largest suburban movie theater in the city of Dallas. It was one of a chain of theaters owned by Howard Hughes. Having many state-of-the-art luxuries, it was the first theater in the city of Dallas to offer its patrons the comfort of air conditioning.

During its lifetime, the theater has seen its share of hardship, switching hands from owner to owner and surviving fire and vandalism. In 2002, restoration commenced and movies were again shown at the theater. Still, most people come to see the chair that Lee Harvey Oswald sat in while in hiding after shooting President

Kennedy. It is painted in gold with the words, "Lee Harvey Oswald, November 22, 1963."

Event prices vary. For normal movie showings, expect to pay a typical movie theater price of $9.50 for adults.

🌐 Frontiers of Flight Museum

6911 Lemmon Ave, Dallas, TX 75235 (Northwest Dallas Love Field)

(214) 350-1651

http://www.flightmuseum.com/

Conveniently located north of downtown on the southeast side of Love Field is the Frontiers of Flight Museum, a place to explore the history, progress, and future of innovation. There are more than 30 aircraft and spacecraft in the museum, some of which were even built in the northern area of Texas.

There are artifacts to get up close to and explore that include a full-sized model of the Wright Flyer from 1903, artifacts from the Hindenburg, and historic representations from World War I, World War II, and the Cold War. There is also a Space Flight gallery with the Apollo 7 on display as well as a moon rock and full-size model of the Soviet Union's Sputnik. Visitors can see two Boeing 737's in the Heart of Our History gallery.

Volunteers are knowledgeable and friendly. Kids with an eye for the sky tend to love the museum as well. It also has a kids' area for them to let off some steam.

The museum is open from 10 a.m. until 5 p.m. on Mondays through Saturdays and from 1 p.m. through 5 p.m. on Sundays. The price for admission is $8 for adults, $6 for seniors (65+), and $5 for children (ages 3-17). Parking is free.

Fair Park

1300 Robert B. Cullum Boulevard, Dallas, TX 75210

(214) 670-8400

http://www.dallascityhall.com/fairpark/coliseum.html

Fair Park is a large urban park that covers more than 227 acres of land (1.12 km^2) and is used as an educational complex as well as nine museums, a lagoon, six performance facilities, and as to host flea markets and other events. It is listed as a National Historic Landmark. It also boasts about having the largest Ferris wheel in

North America. Most of the buildings on the site were built for the Texas Centennial Exposition in 1936 and still stand to this day, serving as a significant example of Art Deco architecture.

On an annual basis, more than 7 million visitors head to Fair Park, 3.5 million of those people come specifically for the Texas State Fair for three weeks every fall. Besides hosting the State Fair, the site also offers year-round activities like the North Texas Irish Festival and Taste of Dallas. Permanent attractions include the Museum of Nature & Science, the Women's Museum, African-American Museum, Museum of the American Railroad, Texas Discovery Gardens, and the Music Hall. As of 2010, the Children's Aquarium at Fair Park was opened.

If the fair environment is what you're after, you'll be happy to know that from May 2013, it will offer rides, food, and entertainment year-round. There will also be a Top o' Texas Tower with a light and sound show.

Prices and hours of operation are dependent upon specific events.

Fountain Place

1445 Ross Ave, Dallas, TX (Downtown Dallas)

(214) 969-1977

http://www.fountainplace.com/index.html

Fountain Place sits in downtown Dallas and is not just a large building, but an entertainment district with fountains in a small urban park. The building has over 26,000 windows and is one of the heaviest buildings of its size with over 42,000 tons of steel. The unique building, designed by Dan Kiley, has no roof and has window mullions with an internal gutter system that takes rainwater from the top of the building to the bottom, where the fountains are located.

Surrounding the building, you will find a romantic and relaxing area of 172 small fountains and streams. During the evening, it takes on a completely different atmosphere with the fountains illuminated by lights as opposed to the sunlight that graces the fountains during the daytime hours. Be warned not to touch or swim in the fountains, however, as security is strictly enforced. Within a few blocks, its arts district is home to over 80 restaurants, 20 arts and entertainment venues, and 12 hotels; making Fountain Place a popular destination for tourists and Dallas residents alike.

🌐 Cowboys Stadium

1 Legends Way, Arlington, TX 76011

(817) 892-4000

http://stadium.dallascowboys.com/

Home of the famous Dallas Cowboys football team, Cowboys Stadium is located just a half hour away from Dallas in Arlington, Texas. Seating 85,000 people, it is the third largest stadium in the National Football League. It is also a newer stadium, replacing the old Texas Stadium in 2009. It now boasts the title of the largest domed stadium in the world with the largest column-free interior. It hosts not only the Dallas Cowboys games in the winter, but also concerts, soccer matches, basketball games, and more.

Unfortunately, due to its location in Arlington, there is no form of public transportation leading to the site. For this reason, it is criticized as the only such stadium in the nation. Car or private shuttles provide the only mode of transportation to the stadium.   Still, the Dallas Cowboys are considered to be "America's Team" and Cowboys games as well as tours of the stadium are popular amongst visitors. Besides serving as a football field, it hosts a world of facts and figures about the world's largest domed structure, a classroom, and an art museum.

Cowboys Stadium offers daily tours that appeal to people of all ages and interests. There are guided tours, educational tours, and art tours. They last at least an hour long. Prices vary but average $27.50

🌎 Pioneer Plaza

Young and Griffin Streets, Dallas, TX 75202 (Downtown Dallas)

DALLAS TRAVEL GUIDE

(214) 953-1184

When visiting downtown Dallas, a must-see photo opportunity exists in Pioneer Plaza. Located at the intersection of Griffin Street and Young Street, it offers an open space filled with bronze cattle and horse statues, setting the scene for a western stampede.

Located in the Convention Center District, downtown, Pioneer Plaza is a large public park and heavily frequented tourist attraction. The sculptures and plaza were the idea of Trammell Crow, a retail developer who wanted a "Western" style sculpture in the heart of Dallas. He organized a group to donate the sculptures and began the project in 1992, on land donated by the city. The project opened in 1994 and has been popular ever since, although some local artists contested at the time that the sculptures were not an accurate historical representation of the city.

The sculptures are supposed to commemorate the cattle drives that took place during the course of the 19th Century along the Shawnee Trail. Robert Summers was the artist who created the 70 bronze steers and 3 trail riders. With each steer measuring 6 feet in height, the collection together comprises the largest bronze monument in the world of its kind. The dramatic "Western" effect is further enhanced by the native landscaping, limestone cliff, and flowing stream that runs through the area.

Today, the Dallas Convention Center, which is adjacent to the park, maintains the grounds. Pioneer Plaza is the second most visited tourist attraction in downtown Dallas.

It is considered a work in progress, with new cattle

occasionally being added to the herd.

This is a great, free photo opportunity. There is free

parking for an hour.

🌐 Southfork Ranch

3700 Hogge Road, Parker, TX

(972) 442-7800

http://www.southforkranch.com/

If you were a fan of the '80s television series, "Dallas,"

you will enjoy a half hour ride to Parker, Texas for a visit

to Southfork Ranch. In 1978, the ranch was chosen as the

site for the show with its beautiful white mansion, pool,

and ranch-like grounds. During the taping of the show, the

original ranch owner resided there with his family. They

soon realized that the fame associated with the show made it difficult to stay there and maintain their private lifestyle. By 1985, they moved and Southfork became an exclusive tourist attraction and location for special events. At this time, the mansion was open to the public and a large conference center was erected to accommodate the many events.

Tourists from around the world flock to the Southfork Ranch to experience the lifestyle made popular by the Ewing family in the television series. It is open daily for guided tours that showcase memorabilia from the show; including the gun that shot J.R., the "Dallas" family tree, Lucy's wedding dress, and Jock's Lincoln Continental. Miss Ellie's Deli serves hungry visitors and there are two retail stores that offer a diverse selection of gifts and memorabilia.

DALLAS TRAVEL GUIDE

Tours leave every 30-45 minutes and depart from the Visitors Center. They run continuously throughout the day. The ranch is open every day except for Thanksgiving and Christmas from 9 a.m. until 5 p.m.

Admission for adults is $13.50 plus tax. Senior Citizens (60+) pay $11.50 plus tax. Children (6-12) pay $8.50 plus tax.

Budget Tips

 # Accommodation

La Quinta Inn & Suites Dallas, Love Field

8300 John W. Carpenter Fwy.

Dallas, TX 75247

Phone: (214) 414-9000

http://www.lq.com/lq/properties/propertyProfile.do?propId

=6482

The 100 percent non-smoking La Quinta Inn & Suites at

Love Field offers easy access to many to downtown

Dallas (4 miles) and Fort Worth. Accommodations include

a hotel restaurant (Bistro Q), outdoor swimming pool,

fitness center, business center, laundry facilities, and

complementary wireless high-speed internet access.

There is also a free "Bright Side" breakfast included in the rate as well as an airport shuttle. Rates start at $89 per night.

Candlewood Suites Dallas Market Center

7930 North Stemmons Freeway, Dallas, TX 75247

(877) 859-5095

http://www.ihg.com/candlewood/hotels/us/en/dallas

Centrally located in Midtown Dallas is the Candlewood Suites Dallas. It is conveniently located just minutes from Love Field, the Dallas Convention Center, and the Dallas Market Center. The hotel offers free high-speed internet access as well as a fitness center, convenience store, pool, free laundry facilities, and an in-suite kitchen for a "home away from home" experience. Rates start at $82 per night.

Omni Park West

1590 LBJ Freeway

Dallas, Texas 75234

Phone: (972) 869-4300

http://www.omnihotels.com/FindAHotel/DallasParkWest

You can sometimes find a deal at the classy Omni Dallas Hotel at Park West, with rates starting at $100 per night. The hotel is close to the Business District and just a ten minute drive from Dallas/Fort Worth International Airport.

The hotel sits amidst a lush park and lake at Park West. It is 100% non-smoking with complementary five mile shuttle service, high-speed wireless internet, and an outdoor pool.

Hawthorn Suites by Wyndham Dallas Park Central

7880 Alpha Road, Dallas, TX 75240 (Formerly Staybridge Suites)

(800) 337-0200

http://www.hawthorn.com/hotels/texas/dallas/

The Hawthorn Suites is located in the Park Central Business District of North Dallas and caters to both short-term and long-term guests. This hotel knows southern hospitality with its free hot breakfast buffet and Manager's Reception offered in the evenings on Tuesdays through Thursdays. There is an outdoor pool and fitness center as well.

The rooms are either one or two bedroom suites with rates that start at $75.

Sheraton Dallas Galleria

4801 Lyndon B. Johnson Freeway, Dallas, TX 75244

http://www.starwoodhotels.com/sheraton

(972) 661-3600

After a $17 million renovation, the Sheraton Dallas Hotel by the Galleria offers updated amenities in a contemporary space. Only a few blocks away from the Galleria Mall, location is everything. It is also in the center of the Business District in North Dallas.

Whether traveling for business or pleasure, the rooms make guests feel at home with high-speed internet access, fitness center, and an outdoor pool. There is also

free transportation to the Galleria Mall and other local

spots. Rates start at $88 per night.

🌐 Restaurants, Cafés & Bars

Spiral Diner & Bakery

1101 N. Beckley, Dallas, TX

(214) 948-4747

http://www.spiraldiner.com/

Spiral Diner is the success story of a few vegan

restaurateurs who have mastered the art of disguising

comfort food favorites as healthy vegan fare.

They use only organic ingredients when possible and

offer only vegan items. This means no meat, eggs, milk,

honey, and the list goes on. Almost everything you can

order on the menu is made from scratch, on site with only the best organic ingredients. They accomplish all this while keeping prices low and keeping customers coming back.

Do not be afraid to try this place if the word, "vegan" scares you. Many people hardly realize it and it is a local favorite. Spiral Diner & Bakery is open daily at 11 a.m. and closes at 10 p.m. every day except Sunday when they close at 5 p.m. The restaurant is closed on Mondays.

Mike Anderson's BBQ

5410 Harry Hines Blvd, Dallas, TX 75235

(214) 630-0735

http://www.mikeandersonsbbq.com/

When in Dallas, or anywhere in the Southwest, it would

be a shame to avoid trying some good BBQ. Mike

Anderson's is nothing fancy but certainly tasty. They

serve cafeteria style and are only open from 10:30 until

2:30 Mondays through Saturdays. They are closed

Sundays.

Although the lines may seem daunting, they move quickly.

You should expect to wait no more than 20 minutes to sit

down and eat. They also serve a complementary soft-

serve ice cream cone with their dinners.

Kenny's Wood Fired Grill

5000 Belt Line Rd #775, Dallas, TX 75254

(972) 392-9663

http://kennyswoodfiredgrill.com/

Kenny's Wood Fired Grill is styled after a typical 1940s

Chicago-style chophouse with a relaxed but classy atmosphere and that typical wood-fired aroma. They serve seafood and prime cut meats, specializing in New England style seafood. Patrons begin their meals by enjoying the complementary popovers. Their frozen tap system at the bar guarantees perfect martinis every time.

Reservations are recommended. Kenny's is open daily at 11 a.m., closing at 10 p.m. on Sundays and Mondays and at midnight Tuesdays through Saturdays. Prices are very reasonable, topping near $29 for an entrée.

Desperados Mexican Restaurant Uno

4818 Greenville Ave, Dallas, TX 75206-4120

(214) 363-1850

http://www.desperadosrestaurant.com/index.php

Desperados Mexican Restaurant is a local favorite. Their traditional Mexican and Tex-Mex dishes have been pleasing customers for over 35 years. Their historic Greenville Avenue location has been a success since it was first opened by Jorge Levy in 1976. Prices are incredibly reasonable for such quality food and margaritas.

They are open daily at 11 a.m., closing at 9 p.m. on Sundays, 10 p.m. on Mondays through Thursdays, and 11 p.m. Fridays and Saturdays.

Celebrations

4503 W Lovers Ln, Dallas, TX 75209-3197

(214) 351-5681

http://www.celebrationrestaurant.com

Celebrations has been offering Southern-style comfort food in its quaint stone building near Love Field for over four decades. Everything on the menu is made from scratch daily. This means that their menu varies day-to-day depending upon what is fresh and in season.

Prices are a value between 410 and $20. Celebrations opens at 11 a.m. on Sundays, closing at 9:30 p.m. During the rest of the week, they open for lunch and then close for few hours until dinner service which ends at 9:30 p.m. on Mondays through Thursdays and at 10 p.m. on Fridays and Saturdays.

🌐 Shopping

Galleria Dallas

13350 Dallas Pkwy, Dallas, TX 75240

(972) 702-7100

http://www.galleriadallas.com/we-are-dallas/shopping/

Galleria Dallas is an upscale mall and entertainment district located in North Dallas. Besides its over 200 shops and restaurants, it offers an indoor ice skating rink and a hotel: The Westin Galleria. Its glass vaulted ceiling is modeled after the Galleria Vittorio Emanuele II in Milan, Italy.

Galleria Dallas is open daily from 10 a.m. until 9 p.m., except for Sundays when the mall closes at 6 p.m.

NorthPark Center

8687 North Central Expwy, Dallas, TX 75225

(214) 361-6345

http://www.northparkcenter.com/

Shoppers will not want to miss NorthPark Center, dubbed by *Shopping Centers Today* as one of the "7 Retail Wonders of the Modern World."

With over 235 different retailers, legendary department stores, and restaurants, its clientele comes not only from all over the United States but also from around the world.

Its 1.2 million square foot expansion, costing over $250 million in 2006 has made it the new standard of excellence for shopping destinations. Besides its world-class shopping, the mall offers an incredible setting for art, landscaping, and architecture for the enjoyment of its customers' high standards. The shopping center has won numerous awards for its display of 20th Century artwork that covers the 1.4 acre garden, CenterPark Garden. It is here where you can find work from Andy Warhol, Joel Shapiro, James Rosenquist, Beverly Pepper, and more.

NorthPark Center offers a wide variety of dining options from contemporary to gourmet on the go. There is also an AMC movie theater with 15 screens and VIP service. The Center is open from 10 a.m. until 9 p.m. Mondays through Saturdays. On Sundays it is open from noon until 6 p.m.

Antique Row

5013 West Lovers Lane

Dallas, TX 75209

DALLAS TRAVEL GUIDE

(214) 353-0080

http://www.antiquerowdallas.com/index.html

Antique Row, located on West Lovers Lane, is "the" destination in Dallas when looking for unique treasures and authentic antiques.

They have an eclectic mix of antique dealers who are constantly bringing items from abroad, ensuring constant variety. Beautiful European furniture, estate jewelry, and accessories are just a few of the things you can find at Antique Row with its ever-changing inventory.

Antique Row is open from 10 a.m. until 5:30 p.m. Mondays through Saturdays. On Sundays, they are open from 1 p.m. until 5 p.m.

Uptown

2808 McKinney Ave. #100

Dallas, TX 75204

http://www.uptowndallas.net/explore-uptown/shopping

If mall shopping is not your thing, try the eclectic Uptown area on McKinney Avenue. In the area that real estate agents have designated Uptown, a vintage trolley line travels along McKinney Avenue, allowing shoppers to jump off to duck into its many antiques shops, art galleries, furniture stores, restaurants, and specialty shops. The M-Line's restored, vintage trolleys are air-conditioned and heated. They run 365 days a year, providing a safe, reliable, clean, and convenient mode of public transportation at no cost to its passengers in the colorful Uptown Neighborhood. Shop and restaurant

hours vary.

West Village

3699 McKinney Ave., Dallas, TX 75204

(214) 219-1144

http://www.westvillagedallas.com/

Also located in Uptown, but at the north end of McKinney

Avenue, is West Village: a European-style outdoor mall

with chic shops, bars, restaurants, and a movie theater.

The area continues to grow from its original 42 carefully

selected stores and restaurants. It is also home to the

Magnolia Art House Cinema. Uptown's West Village is

often referred to as Dallas' most walkable dining,

shopping, and residential district. It is also served by the

free Historic McKinney Avenue Trolley.

Know Before You Go

Entry Requirements

The Visa Waiver Programme (VWP) allows nationals of selected countries to enter the United States for tourism or certain types of business without requiring a visa. This applies to citizens of the UK, Australia, New Zealand, Canada, Chile, Denmark, Belgium, Austria, Latvia, Estonia, Finland, Italy, Hungary, Iceland, France, Germany, Japan, Spain, Portugal, Norway, Sweden, Slovenia, Slovakia, Switzerland, Brunei, Taiwan, South Korea, Luxemburg, Singapore, Liechtenstein, Monaco, Malta, San Marino, Lithuania, Greece, the Netherlands and the Czech Republic. To qualify, you will also need to have a passport with integrated chip, also known as an e-Passport. The e-Passport symbol has to be clearly displayed on the cover of the passport. This secure method of identification will protect and verify the holder in case of identity theft and other breaches of privacy. There are exceptions. Visitors with a criminal record, serious communicable illness or those who were deported or refused entry on a past occasion will not qualify for the Visa Waiver Program and will need to apply for a visa. Holders of a UK passport who have dual citizenship of Iraq, Iran, Sudan, Syria, Somalia, Libya or Yemen (or those who have travelled to the above countries after 2011) will also need to apply for a visa. A requirement of the Visa Waiver Programme is online registration with the Electronic System for Travel Authorisation (ESTA) at least 72 hours before your travels. When entering the United States, you will be able to skip the custom declaration and proceed directly to an Automated Passport Control (APC) kiosk.

If travelling from a non-qualifying country, you will need a visitor's visa, also known as a non-immigrant visa when entering the United States for visiting friends or family, tourism or medical procedures. It is recommended that you schedule your visa interview at least 60 days before your date of travel. You will need to submit a passport that will be valid for at least 6 months after your intended travel, a birth certificate, a police certificate and color photographs that comply with US visa requirements. Proof of financial support for your stay in the United States is also required.

Health Insurance

Medical procedures are very expensive in the United States and there is no free or subsidized healthcare service. The best strategy would be to organize temporary health insurance for the duration of your stay. You will not need any special vaccinations if visiting the United States as tourists. For an immigration visa, the required immunizations are against hepatitis A and B, measles, mumps, rubella, influenza, polio, tetanus, varicella, meningococcal, pneumococcal, rotavirus, pertussis and influenza type B.

There are several companies that offer short-term health insurance packages for visitors to the United States. Coverage with Inbound USA can be purchased online through their website and offer health insurance for periods from 5 to 364 days. Visitor Secure will provide coverage for accidents and new health complications from 5 days to 2 years, but the cost and care of pre-existing medical conditions and dental care is excluded. Inbound Guest offers similar terms for periods of between 5 and 180 days and will email you a virtual membership card as soon as the contract is finalized. Physical cards will be available within one business day of arrival to the United States.

Traveling with Pets

The United States accepts EU pet passports as valid documentation for pets in transit, provided that your pet is up to date on vaccinations. In most instances, the airline you use will require a health certificate. While microchipping is not required, it may be helpful in case your pet gets lost. If visiting from a non-English speaking country, be sure to have an English translation of your vet's certificate available for the US authorities to examine. To be cleared for travel, your pet must have a vet's certificate issued no less than 10 days before your date of travel. Pets need to be vaccinated against rabies at least 30 days prior to entry to the United States. If the animal was recently microchipped, the microchipping procedure should have taken place prior to vaccination. In the case of dogs, it is also important that your pet must test negative for screwworm no later than 5 days before your intended arrival in the United States.

In the case of exotic pets such as parrots, turtles and other reptiles, you will need check on the CITES (Convention on International Trade in Endangered Species of Wild Fauna and Flora) status of the breed, to ensure that you will in fact be allowed to enter the United States with your pet. There are restrictions on bringing birds from certain countries and a quarantine period of 30 days also applies for birds, such as parrots. It is recommended that birds should enter the United States at New York, Los Angeles or Miami, where quarantine facilities are available. The owner of the bird will carry the expense of the quarantine and advance reservations need to be made for this, to prevent the bird being refused entry altogether. Additionally, you will need to submit documentation in the form of a USDA import permit as well as a health certificate issued by your veterinarian less than 30 days prior to the date of entry.

Airports

Your trip will probably be via one of the country's major gateway airports. **Hartsfield–Jackson Atlanta International Airport** (ATL), which is located less than 12km from the central business area of Atlanta in Georgia is the busiest airport in the United States and the world. It processes about 100 million passengers annually. Internationally, it offers connections to Paris, London, Frankfurt Amsterdam, Dubai, Tokyo, Mexico City and Johannesburg. Domestically, its busiest routes are to Florida, New York, Los Angeles, Dallas and Chicago. Delta Airlines maintains a huge presence at the airport, with the largest hub to be found anywhere in the world and a schedule of almost a thousand daily flights. Via a railway station, the airport provides easy access to the city.

Los Angeles International Airport (LAX) is the second busiest airport in the United States and the largest airport in the state of California. Located in the southwestern part of Los Angeles about 24km from the city center, it is easily accessibly by road and rail. Its nine passenger terminals are connected through a shuttle service. Los Angeles International Airport is a significant origin-and-destination airport for travellers to and from the United States. The second busiest airport in California is **San Francisco International Airport** (SFO) and, like Los Angeles it is an important gateway for trans-Pacific connections. It serves as an important maintenance hub for United and is home to an aviation museum. Anyone who is serious about green policies and environmentally friendly alternatives will love San Francisco's airport. There is a special bicycle route to the airport, designated bicycle parking zones and even a service that offers special freight units for travelling with your bicycle. Bicycles are also allowed on its Airtrain service. The third airport of note in California is **San Diego International Airport** (SAN).

Chicago O'Hare International Airport (ORD) is located about 27km northwest of Chicago's central business district, also known as the Chicago Loop. As a gateway to Chicago and the Great Lakes region, it is the US airport that sees the highest frequency of arrivals and departures. Terminal 5 is used for all international arrivals and most international departures, with the exception of Air Canada and some airline carriers under the Star Alliance or Oneworld brand. The Airport Transit System provides easy access for passengers between terminals and to the remote sections of the parking area.

DALLAS TRAVEL GUIDE

Located roughly halfway between the cities of Dallas and Fort Worth, **Dallas-Fort Worth International Airport** (DFW) is the primary international airport serving the state of Texas. Both in terms of passenger numbers and air traffic statistics, it ranks among the ten busiest airports in the world. It is also home to the second largest hub in the world, that of American Airlines, which is headquartered in Texas. Through 8 Interstate highways and 3 major rail services, it provides access to the city centers of both Dallas and Fort Worth, as well as the rest of Texas. An automated people mover, known as the Skylink makes it effortless for passenger to transverse between different sections of the airport and the parking areas. Terminal D is its international terminal. The second busiest airport in Texas is the **George Bush Intercontinental Airport** (IAH) in Houston, which offers connections to destinations across the United States, as well as Mexico, Canada, the Americas and selected cities in Europe and Asia.

John F. Kennedy International Airport (JFK) is located in the neighborhood of Queens. In terms of international passengers, it is one of the busiest airports in the United States, with connections to 6 continents and with the air traffic of 70 different airlines. Its busiest routes are to London, Paris, Los Angeles and San Francisco. It serves as a gateway hub for both Delta and American Airlines. Terminal 8, its newest terminal, is larger than Central Park. It has the capacity of processing around 1600 passengers per hour. An elevated railway service, the Airtrain provides access to all 8 of its terminals and also connects to the Long Island railroad as well as the New York City Subway in Queens. Within the airport, the service is free. Three other major airports also service the New York City area. **Newark Liberty International Airport** (EWR) is New York's second busiest airport and home of the world's third largest hub, that of United Airlines. Newark is located about 24km from Mid Manhattan, between Newark and Elizabeth. Its airtrain offers an easy way of commuting around the airport and connects via the Newark Liberty International Airport Station to the North Jersey Coast line and Northeast Corridor line. Other airports in New York are **La Guardia Airport** (LGA), located on the Flushing Bay Waterfront in Queens and **Teterboro Airport** (TEB), which is mainly used by private charter companies.

Washington D.C. is served by two airports, **Baltimore-Washington International Airport** (BWI) and **Washington Dulles International Airport** (IAD). Other important airports on the eastern side of the United States include **Logan International Airport** (BOS) in Boston, **Philadelphia International Airport** (PHL) and **Charlotte Douglas International Airport** (CLT) in North Carolina. The three busiest airports in the state of Florida are **Miami International Airport** (MIA), **Fort Lauderdale-Hollywood International**

Airport (FLL) and **Tampa International Airport** (TPA). In the western part of the United States, **McCarran International Airport** (LAS) in Las Vegas and **Phoenix Sky Harbor International** (PHX) in Arizona offer important connections. **Denver International Airport** (DEN) in Colorado is the primary entry point to Rocky Mountains, while **Seattle-Tacoma International Airport** (SEA) in Washington State and **Portland International Airport** (PDX) in Oregon provide access to the Pacific Northwest. **Honolulu International Airport** (HNL) is the primary point of entry to Hawaii.

Airlines

The largest air carriers in the United States are United Airlines, American Airlines and Delta Airlines. Each of these could lay claim to the title of largest airline using different criteria. In terms of passenger numbers, Delta Airlines is the largest airline carrier. It was founded from humble beginnings as a crop dusting outfit in the 1920s, but grew to an enormous operation through mergers with Northeast Airlines in the 1970s, Western Airlines in the 1980s and North-western Airlines in 2010. Delta also absorbed a portion of Pan Am's assets and business, following its bankruptcy in the early 1990s. Delta Airlines operates Delta Connections, a regional service covering North American destinations in Canada, Mexico and the United

States. In terms of destinations, United Airlines is the largest airline in the United States and the world. Its origins lie in an early airline created by Boeing in the 1920s, but the company grew from a series of acquisitions and mergers - most recently with Continental Airlines - to its current status as a leading airline. Regional services are operated under the brand United Express, in partnership with a range of feeder carriers including CapeAir, CommutAir, ExpressJet, GoJet Airlines, Mesa Airlines, Republic Airlines, Shuttle America, SkyWest Airlines and Trans State Airlines. American Airlines commands the largest fleet in the United States. It originated from the merger of over 80 tiny regional airlines in the 1930s and has subsequently merged with Trans Caribbean Airways, Air California, Reno Air, Trans World Airlines and, most recently, US Airways. Through the Oneworld Airline Alliance, American Airlines is partnered with British Airways, Finnair, Iberia and Japan Airlines. Regional connections are operated under the American Eagle brand name and include the services of Envoy Air, Piedmont Airlines, Air Wisconsin, SkyWest Airlines, Republic Airlines and PSA Airlines. American Airlines operates the American Airlines Shuttle, a service that connects the cities of New York, Boston and Washington DC with hourly flights on weekdays.

Based in Dallas, Texas, Southwest Airlines is the world's largest budget airline. It carries the highest number of domestic passengers in the United States and operates over 200 daily flights on its 3 busiest routes, namely Chicago, Washington and Las Vegas. JetBlue Airways is a budget airline based in Long Island that operates mainly in the Americas and the Caribbean. It covers 97 destinations in the United States, Mexico, Costa Rica, Puerto Rico, Grenada, Peru, Colombia, Bermuda, Jamaica, the Bahamas, Barbados, the Dominican Republic and Trinidad and Tobago. Spirit Airlines is an ultra low cost carrier which offers flights to destinations in the United States, Latin America, Mexico and the Caribbean. It is based in Miramar, Florida.

Alaska Airlines was founded in the 1930s to offer connections in the Pacific Northwest, but began to expand from the 1990s to include destinations east of the Rocky Mountains as well as connections to the extreme eastern part of Russia. Alaska Airlines recently acquired the brand, Virgin America which represents the Virgin brand in the United States. Silver Airways is a regional service which offers connections to various destinations in Florida, Pennsylvania, Virginia and West Virginia and provides a service to several islands within the Bahamas. Frontier Airlines is a relatively new budget airline that is mainly focussed on connections around the Rocky Mountain states. Hawaiian Airlines is based in Honolulu and offers connections to the American mainland as well as to Asia. Island Air also serves Hawaii and enjoys a partnership with

United Airlines. Mokulele Airlines is a small airline based in Kona Island. It provides access to some of the smaller airports in the Hawaiian Islands. Sun Country Airlines is based in Minneapolis and covers destinations in the United States, Mexico, Costa Rica, Puerto Rica, Jamaica, St Maarten and the US Virgin Islands. Great Lakes Airline is a major participant in the Essential Air Service, a government programme set up to ensure that small and remote communities can be reached by air, following the deregulation of certified airlines. These regional connections include destinations in Arizona, Colorado, Kansas, Minnesota, Nebraska, New Mexico, South Dakota and Wyoming. In the past, Great Lakes Airline had covered a wide range of destinations as a partner under the United Express banner.

☺ Hubs

Hartsfield Jackson Atlanta International Airport serves as the largest hub and headquarters of Delta Airlines. John F. Kennedy International Airport serves as a major hub for Delta's traffic to and from the European continent. Los Angeles International Airport serves as a hub for Delta Airline's connections to Mexico, Hawaii and Japan, but also serves the Florida-California route. Detroit Metropolitan Wayne County Airport is

Delta's second largest hubs and serves as a gateway for connections to Asia.

Washington Dulles International Airport serves as a hub for United Airlines as well as Silver Airways. United Airlines also use Denver International Airport, George Bush Intercontinental Airport in Houston, Los Angeles International Airport, San Francisco International Airport, Newark Liberty International Airport and O'Hare International Airport in Chicago as hubs.

Dallas/Fort Worth International Airport serves as the primary hub for American Airlines. Its second largest hub in the southeastern part of the US is Charlotte Douglas International Airport in North Carolina and its largest hub in the north is O'Hare International Airport in Chicago. Other hubs for American Airlines are Phoenix Sky Harbor International Airport - its largest hub in the west - Miami International Airport, Ronald Reagan Washington National Airport, Los Angeles International Airport, John F Kennedy International Airport in New York, which serves as a key hub for European air traffic and La Guardia Airport also in New York.

Seattle-Tacoma International Airport serves as a primary hub for Alaska Airlines. Other hubs for Alaska include Portland International Airport, Los Angeles International Airport and Ted Stevens - Anchorage International Airport. Virgin America operates a primary hub at San Francisco International Airport, but also has a second hub at Los Angeles International Airport as well as a significant presence at Dallas Love Field. Denver International Airport is the primary hub for Frontier Airlines, which also has hubs at Chicago O'Hare International Airport and Orlando International Airport. Frontier also maintains a strong presence at Hartsfield-Jackson Atlanta International Airport, Cincinnati/North Kentucky International Airport, Cleveland Hopkins International Airport, McCarran International Airport in Las Vegas and Philadelphia International Airport. Honolulu International Airport and Kahului Airport serve as hubs for Hawaiian Airlines. Mokulele Airlines uses Kona International Airport and Kahului Airport as hubs. Minneapolis–Saint Paul International Airport serves as a hub for Delta Airlines, Great Lakes Airlines and Sun Country Airlines. Silver Airways uses Fort Lauderdale-Hollywood International Airport as a primary hub and also has hubs at Tampa International Airport, Orlando International Airport and Washington Dulles International Airport.

Seaports

The Port of Miami is often described as the cruise capital of the world, but it also serves as a cargo gateway to the United States. There are 8 passenger terminals and the Port Miami Tunnel, an undersea tunnel connects the port to the Interstate 95 via the Dolphin Expressway. Miami is an important base for several of the world's most prominent cruise lines, including Norwegian Cruise Lines, Celebrity Cruises, Royal Caribbean International and Carnival Cruises. In total, over 40 cruise ships representing 18 different cruise brands are berthed at Miami. Well over 4 million passengers are processed here annually. There are two other important ports in the state of Florida. Port Everglades is the third busiest cruise terminal in Florida, as well as its busiest cargo terminal. It is home to *Allure of the Seas* and *Oasis of the Seas*, two of the world's largest cruise ships. Oceanfront condominium dwellers often bid ships farewell with a friendly cacophony of horns and bells. The third important cruise port in Florida is Port Canaveral, which has 5 cruise terminals.

With its location on the Mississippi river, New Orleans is an important cargo port, but it also has a modern cruise terminal with over 50 check-in counters. The Port of Seattle is operated by the same organization that runs the city's airport. It has two busy cruise terminals. The Port of Los Angeles has a state of the art World Cruise Center, with three berths for passenger liners. As the oldest port on the Gulf of Mexico, the Port of Galveston dates back to the days when Texas was still part of Mexico. Galveston serves both as a cargo port and cruise terminal.

Money Matters

Currency

The currency of the United States is US dollar (USD). Notes are issued in denominations of $1, $2, $5, $10, $20, $50 and $100. Coins are issued in denominations of $1 (known as a silver dollar, 50c (known as a half dollar), 25c (quarter), 10c (dime), 5c (nickel) and 1c (penny).

Banking/ATMs

ATM machines are widely distributed across the United States and are compatible with major networks such as Cirrus and Plus for international bank transactions. Most debit cards will display a Visa or MasterCard affiliation, which means that you may be able to use them as a credit card as well. A transaction fee will be charged for withdrawals, but customers of certain bank groups such as Deutsche Bank and Barclays, can be charged smaller transaction fees or none at all, when using the ATM machines of Bank of America. While banking hours will vary, depending on the location and banking group, you can generally expect most banks to be open between 8.30am and 5pm. You will be asked for ID in the form of a passport, when using your debit card for over-the-counter transactions.

While you cannot open a bank account in the United States without a social security number, you may want to consider obtaining a pre-paid debit card, where a fixed amount can be pre-loaded. This service is available from various credit card companies in the United States. The American Express card is called Serve and can be used with a mobile app. You can load more cash at outlets of Walmart, CVS Pharmacy, Dollar General, Family Dollar, Rite Aid and participating 7/Eleven stores.

Credit Cards

Credit cards are widely used in the United States and the the major cards - MasterCard, Visa, American Express and Diners Club – are commonly accepted. A credit card is essential in paying for hotel accommodation or car rental. As a visitor, you may want to check about the fees levied on your card for foreign exchange transactions. While Europe and the UK have already converted to chip-and-pin credit card, the transition is still in progress in the United States. Efforts are being made to make the credit cards of most US stores compliant with chip-and-pin technology. You may find that many stores still employ the older protocols at point-of-sales. Be sure to inform your bank or credit card vendor of your travel plans before leaving home.

🌎 Tourist Tax

In the United States, tourist tax varies from city to city, and can be charged not only on accommodation, but also restaurant bills, car rental and other services that cater mainly to tourists. In 22 states, some form of state wide tax is charged for accommodation and 38 states levy a tax on car rental. The city that levies the highest tax bill is Chicago. Apart from a flat fee of $2.75, you can expect to be charged 16 percent per day on hotel accommodation as well as nearly 25% for car rentals. New York charges an 18 percent hotel tax, as does Nashville, while Kansas City, Houston and Indianapolis levy around 17 percent per day hotel tax. Expect to pay 16.5 percent tax per day on your hotel bill in Cleveland and 15.6 percent per day in Seattle, with a 2 percent hike, if staying in the Seattle Tourism Improvement Area. Las Vegas charges 12 percent hotel tax. In Los Angeles, you will be charged a whopping 14 percent on your hotel room, but in Burbank, California, the rate is only 2 percent. Dallas, Texas only charges 2 percent on hotels with more than a hundred rooms. In Portland a city tax of 6 percent is added to a county tax of 5.5 percent. Do inquire about the hotel tax rate in the city where you intend to stay, when booking your accommodation.

☾ Sales Tax

In the United States, the sales tax rate is set at state level, but in most states local counties can set an additional surtax. In some states, groceries and/or prescription drugs will be exempt from tax or charged at a lower rate. There are only five states that charge no state sales tax at all. They are Oregon, Delaware, New Hampshire, Alaska and Montana. Alaska allows a local tax rate not exceeding 7 percent and in Montana, local authorities are enabled to set a surtax rate, should they wish to do so. The state sales tax is generally set at between 4 percent (Alabama, Georgia, Louisiana, and Wyoming) and 7 percent (Indiana, Mississippi, New Jersey, Tennessee, Rhode Island) although there are exceptions outside that spectrum with Colorado at 2.8 percent and California at 7.5 percent. The local surcharge can be anything from 4.7 percent (Hawaii) to around 11 percent (Oklahoma and Louisiana). Can you claim back tax on your US purchases as a tourist? In the United States, sales tax is added retro-actively upon payment, which means that it will not be included in the marked price of the goods you buy. Because it is set at state, rather than federal level, it is usually not refundable.

Two states do offer sales tax refunds to tourists. In Texas you will be able to get tax back from over 6000 participating stores if the tax amount came to more than $12 and the goods were purchased within 30 days of your departure. To qualify, you need to submit the original sales receipts, your passport, flight or transport information and visa details. Refunds are made in cash, cheque or via PayPal. Louisiana was the first state to introduce tax refunds for tourists. To qualify there, you must submit all sales receipts, together with your passport and flight ticket at a Refund Center outlet.

Tipping

Tipping is very common in the United States. In sit-down restaurants, a tip of between 10 and 15 percent of the bill is customary. At many restaurants, the salaries of waiting staff will be well below minimum wage levels. With large groups of diners, the restaurant may charge a mandatory gratuity, which is automatically included in the bill. At the trendiest New York restaurants, a tip of 25 percent may be expected. While you can add a credit card tip, the best way to ensure the gratuity reaches your server is to tip separately in cash. Although tipping is less of an obligation at takeaway restaurants, such as McDonalds, you can leave your change, or otherwise $1, if there is a tip jar on the counter. In the case of pizza delivery, a minimum of $3 is recommended and more is obviously appreciated. Although a delivery charge is often levied, this money usually goes to the pizzeria, rather than the driver. Tip a taxi driver 10 percent of the total fare. At your hotel, tip the porter between $1 and $2 per bag. Tip between 10 and 20 percent at hair salons, spas, beauty salons and barber shops. Tip tour guides between 10 and 20 percent for a short excursion. For a day trip, tip both the guide and the driver $5 to $10 per person, if a gratuity is not included in the cost of the tour. Tip the drivers of charter or sightseeing buses around $1 per person.

Connectivity

Mobile Phones

There are four major service providers for wireless connection in the United States. They are Verizon Wireless, T-Mobile US, AT&T Mobility and Sprint. Not all are compatible with European standards. While most countries in Europe, Asia, the Middle East and East Africa uses the GSM mobile network, only two US service providers, T-Mobile and AT&T Mobility aligns with this. Also bear in mind that GSM carriers in the United States operate using the 850 MHz/1900 MHz frequency bands, whereas the UK, all of Europe, Asia, Australia and Africa use 900/1800MHz. You should check with your phone's tech specifications to find out whether it supports these standards. The other services, Verizon Wireless and Sprint use the CDMA network standard and, while Verizon's LTE frequencies are somewhat compatible with those of T-Mobile and AT&T, Sprint uses a different bandwidth for its LTE coverage.

To use your own phone, you can purchase a T-Mobile 3-in-1 starter kit for $20. If your device is unlocked, GMS-capable and supports either Band II (1900 MHz) or Band IV (1700/2100 MHz), you will be able to access the T-Mobile network. You can also purchase an AT&T sim card through the Go Phone Pay-as-you-go plan for as little as $0.99. Refill cards are available from $25 and are valid for 90 days. If you want to widen your network options, you may want to explore the market for a throwaway or disposable phone. At Walmart, you can buy non-contracted phones for as little as $9.99, as well as pre-paid sim cards and data top-up packages.

Canadians travellers will find the switch to US networks technically effortless, but should watch out for roaming costs. Several American networks do offer special international rates for calls to Canada or Mexico.

DALLAS TRAVEL GUIDE

Dialing Code

The international dialing code for the United States is +1.

Emergency Numbers

General Emergency: 911 (this number can be used free of charge from any public phone in the United States).
MasterCard: 1-800-307-7309
Visa: 1-800-847-2911

General Information

Public Holidays

1 January: New Year's Day

3rd Monday in January: Martin Luther King Day

3rd Monday in February: President's Day

Last Monday in May: Memorial Day

4 July: Independence Day

1st Monday in September: Labour Day

2nd Monday in October: Columbus Day

11 November: Veteran's Day

4th Thursday in November: Thanksgiving Day

4th Friday in November: Day after Thanksgiving

25 December: Christmas Day (if Christmas Day falls on a Sunday, the Monday thereafter is a public holiday.) In some states, 26 December is a public holiday as well.

There are several festivals that are not public holidays per se, but are culturally observed in the United States. They include:

14 February: Valentine's Day

17 March: St Patrick's Day

March/April (variable): Easter or Passover

Second Sunday in May: Mother's Day

3rd Sunday in June: Father's Day

31 October: Halloween

Time Zones

The United States has 6 different time zones. **Eastern Standard Time** is observed in the states of Maine, New York, New Hampshire, Delaware, Vermont, Maryland, Rhode Island, Massachusetts, Connecticut, Pennsylvania, Ohio, North Carolina, South Carolina, Georgia, Virginia, West Virginia, Michigan, most of Florida and Indiana as well as the eastern parts of Kentucky and Tennessee. Eastern Standard Time is calculated as Greenwich Meantime/Coordinated Universal Time (UTC) -5. **Central Standard Time** is observed in Iowa, Illinois, Missouri, Arkansas, Louisiana, Oklahoma, Kansas,

Mississippi, Alabama, near all of Texas, the western half of Kentucky, the central and western part of Tennessee, sections of the north-western and south-western part of Indiana, most of North and South Dakota, the eastern and central part of Nebraska and the north-western strip of Florida, also known as the Florida Panhandle. Central Standard Time is calculated as Greenwich Meantime/Coordinated Universal Time (UTC) -6.

Mountain Standard Time is observed in New Mexico, Colorado, Wyoming, Montana, Utah, Arizona, the southern and central section of Idaho, the western parts of Nebraska, South Dakota and North Dakota, a portion of eastern Oregon and the counties of El Paso and Hudspeth in Texas. Mountain Standard Time is calculated as Greenwich Meantime/Coordinated Universal Time (UTC) -7. **Pacific Standard Time** is used in California, Washington, Nevada, most of Oregon and the northern part of Idaho. Pacific Standard Time is calculated as Greenwich Meantime/Coordinated Universal Time (UTC) -8.

Alaska Standard Time is used in Alaska and this can be calculated as Greenwich Meantime/Coordinated Universal Time (UTC) -9. Because of its distant location, Hawaii is in a time zone of its own. **Hawaii Standard Time** can be calculated as Greenwich Meantime/Coordinated Universal Time (UTC) -10.

DALLAS TRAVEL GUIDE

🌏 Daylight Savings Time

Clocks are set forward one hour at 2.00am on the second Sunday of March and set back one hour at 2.00am on the first Sunday of November for Daylight Savings Time. The states of Hawaii and Arizona do not observe Daylight Savings Time. However, the Navajo Indian Reservation, which extends across three states (Arizona, Utah and New Mexico), does observe Daylight Savings Time throughout its lands, including that portion which falls within Arizona.

🌏 School Holidays

In the United States, the academic year begins in September, usually in the week just before or after Labour Day and ends in the early or middle part of June. There is a Winter Break that includes Christmas and New Year and a Spring Break in March or April that coincides with Easter. In some states, there is also a Winter Break in February. The summer break occurs in the 10 to 11 weeks between the ending of one academic year and the commencement of the next academic year. Holidays may vary according to state and certain weather conditions such as hurricanes or snowfall may also lead to temporary school closures in affected areas.

DALLAS TRAVEL GUIDE

☯ Trading Hours

Trading hours in the United States vary. Large superstores like Walmart trade round the clock at many of its outlets, or else between 7am and 10pm. Kmart is often open from 8am to 10pm, 7 days a week. Target generally opens at 8am and may close at 10 or 11pm, depending on the area. Many malls will open at 10am and close at 9pm. Expect restaurants to be open from about 11am to 10pm or 11pm, although the hours of eateries that serve alcohol and bars may be restricted by local legislation. Banking hours also vary, according to branch and area. Branches of the Bank of America will generally open at 9am, and closing time can be anywhere between 4pm and 6pm. Most post office outlets are open from 9am to 5pm on weekdays.

☯ Driving

In the United States, motorists drive on the right hand side of the road. As public transport options are not always adequate, having access to a car is virtually essential, when visiting the United States. To drive, you will need a valid driver's licence from your own country, in addition to an international driving permit. If your driver's licence does not include a photograph, you will be asked to submit your passport for identification as well.

For car rental, you will also need a credit card. Some companies do not rent out vehicles to drivers under the age of 25. Visitors with a UK license may need to obtain a check code for rental companies, should they wish to verify the details and validity of their driver's licence, via the DVLA view-your-licence service. This can also be generated online, but must be done at least 72 hours prior to renting the car. In most cases, though, the photo card type license will be enough. The largest rental companies - Alamo, Avis, Budget, Hertz, Dollar and Thrifty - are well represented in most major cities and usually have offices at international airports. Do check about the extent of cover included in your travel insurance package and credit card agreement. Some credit card companies may include Collision Damage Waiver (CDW), which will cover you against being held accountable for any damage to the rental car, but it is recommended that you also arrange for personal accident insurance, out-of-state insurance and supplementary liability insurance. You can sometimes cut costs on car rentals by reserving a car via the internet before leaving home.

The maximum speed limit in the United States varies according to state, but is usually between 100km per hour (65 m.p.h.) and 120km per hour (75 m.p.h.). For most of the Eastern states, as well as California and Oregon on the west coast the maximum speed driven on interstate highways should be 110km per hour (70 m.p.h.). Urban speed legislation varies, but in business and residential areas, speeds are usually set between 32km (20 miles) and 48km (30 miles) per hour. In Colorado, nighttime speed limits apply in certain areas where migrating wildlife could be endangered and on narrow, winding mountain passes, a limit of 32km (20 miles) per hour sometimes applies. In most American states there is a ban on texting for all drivers and a ban on all cell phone use for novice drivers.

Drinking

It is illegal in all 50 states for persons under the age of 21 to purchase alcohol or to be intoxicated. In certain states, such as Texas, persons between the age of 18 and 21 may be allowed to drink beer or wine, if in the company of a parent or legal guardian. In most states, the trading hours for establishments selling alcohol is limited. There are a few exceptions to this. In Nevada, alcohol may be sold round the clock and with few restrictions other than age. In Louisiana, there are no restrictions on trading in alcohol at state level, although some counties set their own restrictions. By contrast, Arizona has some of the strictest laws in relation to alcohol sales, consumption and driving under the influence. The sale of alcohol is prohibited on Native American reservations, unless the tribal council of that reservation has passed a vote to lift restrictions.

☻ Smoking

There is no smoking ban set at federal level in the United States. At state level, there are 40 states in total that enact some form of state wide restriction on smoking, although the exemptions of individual states may vary. In Arizona, California, Colorado, Connecticut, Delaware, Hawaii, Illinois, Iowa, Kansas, Maine, Maryland, Massachusetts, Michigan, Minnesota, Montana, Nebraska, North Dakota, New Jersey, New Mexico, New York, Ohio, Oregon, Rhode Island, South Dakota, Utah, Vermont, Washington and Wisconsin, smoking is prohibited in all public enclosed areas, including bars and restaurants. The states of Arkansas, Florida, Indiana, Louisiana, Pennsylvania and Tennessee do have a general state wide restriction on smoking in public places, but exempt adult venues where under 21s are not allowed. This includes bars, restaurants, betting shops and gaming parlours (Indiana) and casinos (Louisiana and Pennsylvania). Nevada also has a state wide ban on smoking that exempts casinos, bars, strip clubs and brothels. In Georgia, state wide smoking legislation exempts bars and restaurants that only serve patrons over the age of 18. Idaho has a state wide ban that includes restaurants, but exempts bars serving only alcohol. New Hampshire, North Carolina and Virginia have also introduced some form of state wide smoking restriction. While the states of Alabama, Alaska, Kentucky, Mississippi, Missouri, Oklahoma, South Carolina, Texas, West Virginia and Wyoming have no state legislation, there are more specific restrictions at city and county level. In Arizona, there is an exemption for businesses located on Native American reservation and, in particular, for Native American religious ceremonies that may include smoking rituals. In California, the first state to implement anti-smoking legislation, smoking is also prohibited in parks and on sidewalks.

Electricity

Electricity: 110 volts

Frequency: 60 Hz

Electricity sockets are compatible with American Type A and Type B plugs. The Type A plug features two flat prongs or blades, while the Type B plug has the same plus an additional 'earth' prong. Most newer models of camcorders and cameras are dual voltage, which means that you should be able to charge them without an adapter in the United States, as they have a built in converter for voltage. You may find that appliances from the UK or Europe which were designed to accommodate a higher voltage will not function as effectively in the United

States. While a current converter or transformer will be able to adjust the voltage, you may still experience some difficulty with the type of devices that are sensitive to variations in frequency as the United States uses 60 Hz, instead of the 50 Hz which is common in Europe and the UK. Appliances like hairdryers will usually be available in hotels and since electronic goods are fairly cheap in the United States, the easiest strategy may be to simply purchase a replacement. Bear in mind, that you may need an adaptor or transformer to operate it once you return home.

🌐 Food & Drink

Hamburgers, hot dogs and apple pie may be food items that come to mind when considering US culinary stereotypes, but Americans eat a wide variety of foods. They love steaks and ribs when dining out and pancakes or waffles for breakfast. As a society which embraces various immigrant communities, America excels at adopting and adapting traditional staples and adding its own touch to them. Several "Asian" favorites really originated in the United States. These include the California roll (offered in sushi restaurants) and the fortune cookie (chinese). Popular Hispanic imports include tacos, enchiladas and burritos. Another stereotype of American cuisine is large portion sizes. Hence the existence of American inventions such as the footlong sub, the footlong chilli cheese hot dog and the Krispy Creme burger, which combines a regular hamburger with a donut. Corn dogs are fairground favorites. Most menus are more balanced however. It is common to ask for a doggy bag (to take away remaining food) in a restaurant.

When in the South, enjoy corn bread, grits and southern fried chicken. Try spicy buffalo wings in New York, traditionally prepared baked beans in Boston and deep dish pizza in Chicago. French fries are favorites with kids of all ages, but Americans also love their potatoes as hash browns or the bite sized tater tots. Indulge your sweet tooth with Twinkies, pop tarts, cup cakes and banana splits. Popular sandwiches include the BLT (bacon, lettuce, tomato, the Reuben sandwich, the sloppy joe and the peanut butter and jelly.

Sodas (fizzy drinks) and bottled waters are the top beverages in the United States. The top selling soft drinks are Coca Cola, followed by Pepsi Cola, Diet Coke, Mountain Dew and Dr Pepper. In America's colonial past, tea was initially the hot beverage of choice and it was tea politics that kicked off the American Revolution, but gradually tea has been replaced by coffee in popularity. From the 1970s, Starbucks popularized coffee culture in the United States. Americans still drink gallons of tea and they are particularly fond of a refreshing glass of iced tea. Generally, Americans drink more beer than wine and favorite brands include Bud Light, followed by Coors Light, Budweiser and Miller Light. Popular cocktails are the Martini, the Manhattan, the Margarita, the Bloody Mary, the Long Island Ice tea and Sex on the Beach.

American Sports

Baseball is widely regarded as the national sport of America. The sport originated in the mid 1800s and superficially shares the basic objective of cricket, which is to score runs by hitting a ball pitched by the opposing team, but in baseball, the innings ends as soon as three players have been caught out. A point is scored when a runner has passed three bases and reached the 4th or home base of the baseball diamond. After 9 innings, the team with the highest number of runs is declared the winner. The Baseball World Series is played in the fall (autumn), usually in October, and consists of best-of-seven play-off between the two top teams representing the rival affiliations of the National League and American League.

Although the origins of American football can be found in rugby, the sport is now widely differentiated from its roots and today numerous distinctions exist between the two. In American football, a game is divided into four quarters, with each team fielding 11 players, although unlimited substitution is allowed.

Players wear helmets and heavy padding as any player can be tackled, regardless of ball possession. An annual highlight is the Super Bowl, the championship game of the National Football League. The event is televised live to over a 100 million viewers and features a high profile halftime performance by a top music act. Super bowl Sunday traditionally takes place on the first Sunday of February.

The roots of stock car racing can be found in America's prohibition era, when bootleggers needed powerful muscle cars (often with modifications for greater speed) to transport their illicit alcohol stocks. Informal racing evolved to a lively racing scene in Daytona, Florida. An official body, NASCAR, was founded in 1948 to regulate the sport, NASCAR. Today, NASCAR racing has millions of fans. One of its most prestigious events is the Sprint Cup, a championship which comprises of 36 races and kicks off each year with the Daytona 500.

Rodeo originated from the chores and day-to-day activities of Spanish cattle farmers and later, the American ranchers who occupied the former Spanish states such as Texas, California and Arizona. The advent of fencing eliminated the need for cattle drives, but former cowboys found that their skills still offered good entertainment, providing a basis for wild west shows such as those presented by Buffalo Bill. Soon, rodeo events became the highlight of frontier towns throughout the west. During the first half of the 20th centuries, organizations formed to regulate events. Today, rodeo is considered a legitimate national sport with millions of fans. If you want to experience the thrill of this extreme sport, attend one of its top events. The Prescott Frontier Days show in Arizona is billed to be America's oldest rodeo. The Reno Rodeo in Nevada is a 10 day event that takes place in mid-June and includes the option of closer participation as a volunteer. Rodeo Houston, a large 20 day event that takes place towards the end of winter, is coupled to a livestock show. Visit the San Antonio show in Texas during February for the sheer variety of events. The National Western Rodeo in Denver Colorado is an indoor event that attracts up to half a million spectators each year. The National Finals that takes place in Las Vegas during December is the prestigious championship that marks the end of the year's rodeo calendar.

Useful Websites

https://esta.cbp.dhs.gov/esta/ -- The US Electronic System for Travel Authorization
http://www.visittheusa.com/
http://roadtripusa.com/
http://www.roadtripamerica.com/

DALLAS TRAVEL GUIDE

http://www.road-trip-usa.info/

http://www.autotoursusa.com/

http://www.onlyinyourstate.com/

http://www.theamericanroadtripcompany.co.uk/

Printed in Great Britain
by Amazon